HOMUNCULUS

James Womack was born in Cambridge
in 1979. He studied Russian, English and
translation at university, and received his
doctorate, on W.H. Auden's translations, in
2006. He lived in Madrid from 2008 to 2017,
and now teaches Spanish and translation at
Cambridge University. He is a freelance
translator from Russian and Spanish, and
helps run Calque Press, which concentrates
on poetry, translation and the environment.
His debut collection of poems, *Misprint*, was
published by Carcanet in 2012, and *On Trust:
A Book of Lies* came out in 2017.

JAMES WOMACK

# *Homunculus*

CARCANET

First published in Great Britain in 2020 by
Carcanet
Alliance House, 30 Cross Street
Manchester M2 7AQ
www.carcanet.co.uk

A CIP catalogue record for this book is
available from the British Library.

ISBN 978 1 78410 991 2

Book design by Andrew Latimer
Printed in Great Britain by SRP Ltd, Exeter, Devon

The publisher acknowledges financial
assistance from Arts Council England.

# CONTENTS

*for M.*

## TO MAXIMIAN

This Easter, when smoke filled our eyes
from the Great Fire of England,
over the years I reached to you,
expecting at best a handful of ash.
    No, but you did respond: not with consolation,
not that: rather dark-eyed and weary
in the teeth of our eternal similar mistakes.

    (Bear this in mind: I call your book *Homunculus*
because I lack the balls to call it *Sperm*.)

*I, meta-traveller from an antique land...*

I.

I am old.

       Oh fuck,
              I am old.

Life, what have you got against me, life?
Why won't you release me?
What kind of a marriage is this, that I can't escape
when it suits me? Why are you so slow?
I'm done. I'm so, so done with this:
death is instantaneous – I don't fear death –
    *... Dying, on the other hand...*
    Y'know, I'd at least get out of the cage.
I'm past the stage of thinking, when I wake
in the middle of the night, *oh, this is better*
*than not waking in the middle of the night.*
When they abolished the death penalty
they knew what they were doing, the sadists,
to swap that useful noose for eternal jolt-legged decay.
    I'm not the man I once was, in all senses:
I'll break myself down for you but in short,
I was a pretty big deal. You would have heard of me.
And now, however loud I shout, no one hears me:
my voice is cracked and I am ill and I am scared.
    *... Languor and horror...*
Life is boring; are we still allowed to say that?
Life used to be fun; now it is less fun,
and worse than the act of fading away
is my ASAP desire to fade.

OK, here's how it was. When I was young
and hot – let's not forget hot – I was famous,
a speaker transparently loved *dans tout l'univers*.
(If I fall into French, be aware I am building
my life from a foreign translation.)
  When I was young I would lie, lie with sweet
poetic lies, and found I could exchange my fictions
for true glory. I was on fire, possible connections
sparking in my mind like a faulty electric chair.
I knew that if I held my mind right,
tremendous thoughts would illuminate it.
  I took to the law, and won case after case after case.
*My* brain, *my* tongue, *my* thoughts: all of them glorious.
  *... And what of that is left to you, now you are old?...*


As well as my wit, I was – how to put it? – beautiful.
It was almost unfair how many advantages I had.
(I say *almost*, because they were mine, and I used them:
if you had been more handsome and cleverer than I,
now that would have been a fucking tragedy.)
  Beauty's wonderful, useful even if you're a moron.
And I was not a moron, and I was strong,
happy in my beautiful body and mind.
  How did I use all this? Sport: if I rode to hounds,
I would cross fifteen large fields and kill a fox;
if I went trap-shooting, the clays would all explode.
I'd spit the eyes from the Jack of Spades
in any saloon of your choice. Think about the way
this arm moved, my right arm, muscles sliding
over muscles under my soft and flexible skin.
  I never went in for that brand of Turkish wrestling
where one is permitted to stick a greased forefinger
up your opponent's asshole for better purchase,
but, that aside, I tried all forms of unarmed combat.

I could run fast, and no one could run faster.
And, as I said, I was witty and praised for my wit.
  Olympic medals, some talk of a Nobel Prize –
I was magnanimous enough not to care which –
everything working as one, the complete package.
Individually, my talents would have been exceptional:
when they all came together, they were… more than that.
  Oh, and did I mention I was modest?


  I went out in the wind and the rain without a hat,
in ways that I now, rheum and bored, cannot believe.
Too hot? Meh.
Too cold? Meh.
All weather? Meh.
I swam in tsunami residue, swam in the cold Thames,
swam, ideally naked, in the February Neva.
More examples.
               I was king of the power nap:
my batteries full off a ten-minute siesta;
my stamina was incredible (more on this later).
Food: I ate a mouthful of grapes and… boom!
Energy for a week.
  And, if a friend told me I just *had* to go to the pub,
I would go, and drink,
and match the Gods of vodka shot for shot
until pale Bacchus and green-faced Smirnoff
would admit Absolut defeat
and vom or slump under the table:
whichever came first.
  I had a supernova inside me,
a burning, unstoppable core.


  Now for the philosophy bit.
What I was doing was tough:

to bend a soul to such activity is tough,
to live an ascetic and a drunken life is tough,
to keep two paths within one mind is more than tough.
They say that Marx was good at double consciousness,
and Charles de Gaulle, and Socrates, and Cato.
Axiomatically: THERE IS NO SUCH THING AS VICE,
JUST THE INABILITY TO FORCE AN ACTION TO ITS END.
   Choice between two things is always choice between four:
this or that, and, hidden underneath, both or neither.
I understood this early, and I lived
life in this knowledge, balancing extremes
without wobbling, like the tightrope walker
who feels safe with a long stick
and the cataracts beneath him.
I was happy with not much, and needed less.


   And now here you come again, life-in-decay,
cock-blocking my reminiscences.
Only you can get the better of me,
put me in harness, put them all in harness.
Marx, de Gaulle, Socrates and Cato,
all the movers and makers, and here you come,
with your sticky pillows, insidious and horrid,
and your hagfish reminders that this will all go,
that these arms, so firm, will become soft as roux,
the brain, all of it. You will eat yourself
down to dust when you have eaten me.
Oh, here you come again, here you come.


   Everyone hoped that I would get married,
but when I say I was *not the marrying kind*
I don't want you to think I'm euphemising.
I mean, I never signed the temperance pledge:
*lips that touch penis shall never touch mine* &c.,

but I was just… not the marrying kind.
I was having too much fun.
It was better to live free of all ties,
however pleasant, however apparently light.

I would walk through Rome – let's call it Rome,
though all cities are the same and I've lived in them all –
and I was beautiful and my daily walk
was a parade of my beauty. And all the girls,
the ones who were looking for me,
the ones who happened to be looked at by me,
met my eyes and blushed. Labia-red, glans-red.
They would smile and run to hide, not too fast,
making sure I saw them as they ran.

Last night, I read a book about Fragonard,
tried to spark something from the embers.
*Fragonard liked scenes in which a young girl,*
*running, fleeing, or crying out in mock terror,*
*in her flight and in her haste*
*inadvertently reveals one of her breasts.*
And in the margin I wrote *I bet he did.*

But then I cried dry tears a little,
because that, indeed, had been my life,
my real life, and not my life in another's art
two hundred and fifty years ago.


But I have been beautiful, and I used my beauty,
and all the girls saw in me the one
who would be their one, who would extinguish
the flame of their hymen. (This is wrong:
the French text says *le flambeau d'hyménée,*
which, whatever it means, doesn't mean that.
I don't know French any more, and never liked it,
though one word, *pitoyable*, is far superior
to its English equivalent. Not equivalent.)

I fooled around. I told you; I was modest,
and I wanted the whole world, very modestly.
My aim was to marry a beautiful woman,
but the marriage bed remained cold and unused.
    The second-best bed, well, that could tell some stories,
if it could speak, and were not traumatised,
this odd sentient bed, to be so regularly abused…
I tried out the merchandise, discovered my calling:
the *mons veneris*, this was the hill I would die on!

    I found I didn't like thin girls, didn't like fat ones
(oh, I can't resist this other line from the French:
*J'avais en horreur et la maigreur et l'embonpoint* –
they order this matter better, &c. &c.).
I didn't like the giants or the dwarves.
Tall posh girls scared me the most –
even the inevitable erotic fantasies
were flawed, taking those tall, beautiful women
and creating the masturbatory equivalent
of an enthusiastic chihuahua
joggling behind an indifferent Great Dane.
    I liked girls who were well-proportioned,
medium-sized, the happy medium:
it's the golden mean where we find most pleasure,
and, to zoom in a little, the middle of the body
is where one finds… well, you know what I mean.

    *You say vagína, I say vagīna…*
    *Let's call the whole thing muff.*

    This sounds a little bit like judging livestock,
but I'm just sketching out my type.
Your mileage may vary, and who am I
talking to in any case, why are you listening to me

if not for me to spill these particular beans?
 I liked girls who were slender, but not skinny:
no pleasure in the pleasures of the flesh without flesh.
I liked to hold them tight and feel *them*,
not their skeleton digging into my gut.
 Oh, the ironies, when now the next woman
I hold will likely be just such a bony lady,
who will grip me tight in her version of lust
                              and never let me go.


 And I did not like pale-skinned girls.
Except that I did, when their pale skin
could be made to bloom like a rose –
could respond to some clever remark
or compliment just this side of suggestive –
the colour coming up from underneath
like a strawberry bobbing in cream.
There's a dream there somewhere.
 I think this is the perfect colour,
certainly I think it is the colour of love:
why else do we sell so many roses,
if we don't think they are Venus's flower?
 In the matter of hair, I was in favour:
blonde for preference, long better than short;
a yoghurt-white neck and an innocent-seeming face
(the kind of face you scrutinise for the moments
when the inner devil outwits the outer mask).
I would love to watch such a woman eating fish:
the fork slowing as it reaches her mouth,
her pink cat tongue waiting to receive it.
 Eyebrows? Do I have to have an opinion?
Dark, I guess, but I never really went for them.
A clear forehead, eyes like black fires:
these won me over, burnt my defences.

Lips that were full but not overflowing,
ripe not overripe, bee-kissed rather than bee-stung.
Modest lips responding immodestly to my kisses.
And a simple gold chain – *noli me tangere* optional –
was all the adornment a perfect neck required:
gold on such a backdrop shines brighter than gems.
    … Gone, all gone, all gone…


*Roses are red*
*Soon we'll be dead.*


I loved these things, and I was right to do so,
but at some point you have to stop,
if you don't want to be the dirty old man
standing for schoolgirls at the school-gate or the bus-stop:
*By the thumbing of my prick*
*Something naughty this way skips…*
Sad old men, aware of their own decay,
with nothing in their minds to satisfy them,
whose memories swell and slump like the moon.
Lust used to be welcome, and now it is a crime.
    You need to always grow up, do what is right
for now, for you. *Do I need to learn to play dominoes?*
*Very well, I will learn to play dominoes.*
There's nothing so tragic as an aging hipster.


A boy is light-hearted, joyous, and that pleases us:
there is something suspicious about a twelve-year-old
who doesn't eat toffee and who reads the *Financial Times*.
    An older man is serious and that pleases us as well:
we laugh, not too kindly, at desperate tattoos,
the flailingly relevant, their surgeries and trophy girlfriends.
    There's a point where everything is in balance:

the young man, old enough to know what is serious
and young enough not to take any of it seriously.
　　I am breaking the rules: it is best for old men to be silent,
and to leave the children to babble and giggle.


　　Time takes us all. If it's a river,
it's not an academic river; it doesn't wind quiet
through arcades and colonnades,
and high smooth banks.
We are thrown high and low,
bitter spray in our mouths;
we have to deal with rapids and cataracts.
　　We cannot choose which way we float
or even if we reach the finish line
with our heads still above the water.


　　My old age is heavy. I thought
the worst thing about adolescence –
apart from growing into a body
that you had not asked for –
was the stress of realising
this new tiredness,
foreign, immense,
was yours forever.
　　I might have been right, but think about
how it builds in the bones as it builds the bones.
My old age is heavy. My life is heavy, and useless.


　　*One quiet night I was awakened*
*by a regular headboardish thud*
*that went on, and on, and, impressively, on.*
*How selfish of the neighbours*
*to make such a noise, I thought.*

*And I listened and listened.*
*It seemed endless.*
*It was my own heart beating.*

I cannot live, just fucking let me die.

What law is this, what justice:
unhappiness stretched out over time?
I used to think beauty was more beautiful
when it was fleeting, that in the leaps
and arabesques of dancers there was a power
that cut me deeper than any poem.
I held my breath as I watched people dance;
if I'd done the same while I read a book I'd have fainted.
Onstage, the meaning, which was the beauty,
pressed itself into me all in such a short span
that I felt like I had been punched.
And then the beauty faded.
Why can't ugliness be like that?
Why can't all our experiences be temporary,
fading, impossible to reproduce?
Why can't I move beyond a condition I detest?
Why, once again, life, why can't I die?

I'm an old man, but I once was a great seducer:
although I don't have the moves any more
I know what they used to be.
Death is the standoffishest girl in the room,
the one who won't meet your eye,
who ignores your astonishing choreography,
and sends the drink back to the barman.
And then, when the man who wants to live
gets past the bouncer, stands diffidently,
hapless holds his casual Virgin Mary,

Death spins round, smiles her most radiant smile,
and within a minute is doing the mambo.
   Death and life have taken it in turns
to rough me over, bad cop | bad cop,
but they're both so careful. Look at me now:
heading, still alive, step by step, to hell.


   What's that? I'm sorry, my hearing's shot.
And yes, these eyes are clouded and pathetic.
My sense of taste is feeble, and only perks up
at potent beef rendang, or vindaloo,
which cause their own, more embarrassing problems.
   I have entered the soup years, the gruel years,
the years of desperate roughage,
the years of bland and distressing comfort food.
   You'd have thought that touch would remain,
if only to taunt me, the curve of a back
or the swoop of a thigh embedded forever
in these hands. But no, I can't remember touch,
and if you had me touch anything now
I would not be able to tell you what it was.
   Never mind a back or a thigh,
I couldn't figure out a Rubik's cube
or a pair of tweezers.
   Smell still sparks me, maybe. A scent or two
makes its way past my nostril hair
(hair from my balding head
takes thick refuge in my nose):
but what it brings me, once identified,
is more keen regret at all I have lost.
   I was once so obsessed with her perfume
I imagined it as something to drink, or eat:
*a smooth chocolate truffle shell*
*filled with 10ml of her perfume:* Idylle

*by Guerlain, with hints*
*of rose, patchouli and warm white musk, the scents*
*of that one dirty weekend your heart has tried to purify.*
*It burns as it goes down.*
     And the joke of it is that I have forgotten her name.
Laugh, you fuckers, har-de-fucking-har.


     Seriously, if I don't have any of this,
can I still be thought of as one of the living?
I don't think I'm dead, I didn't take the taxi ride
(you know: *South of the Lethe, this time of night?*
He-he. I'm sorry, I don't mean to laugh:
the laughter of old men looks hellish),
but my mind is loose and I might be dead.
No, I might as well be dead, for all the use I am.
     I have forgotten so many things,
and if I end up forgetting myself
that's only one more item on the list.
There's nothing asked of my mind –
I never tried, but I sometimes think
you could hold a candle-flame to the palm of my hand
and I would say nothing, notice nothing, feel nothing.
Mind and body, zimmerframing down the hill together.
Every now and then we pause and count our curses.


     What you're reading here doesn't count:
I have stopped writing poetry.
My songs are stilled, the joy I had in them
vanished like a dancer completing his role.
Why should I care about words any more,
when I can't speak them as they should be spoken?
My voice is wine that has turned to vinegar,
the last ghost of a fine vintage,
fit only for dousing lettuce.

And poetry, because it is full of lies,
is no comfort. When you are young,
you don't notice the lies,
or you think they don't matter,
but you find they do matter, are matter.
My years as a lawyer are done,
except for occasional soft cases
to keep my unfeeling hand in.
My personalised number-plate
reads, in Yiddish, VE I 5 MIR.


I myself am gone. I have waved goodbye
to my beauty, put my beauty into its grave,
and am as dead as it is.
My complexion was a mixture of snow and roses,
and now it is meltwater and lilies, linen and paper,
pale as the vampire death I need to come and take me.
I mentioned my nose;
the rest of me is equally grotesque.
My skin is dry, hardening and loose,
takes minutes to sit back when pinched.
Tendons stand like umbrella struts beneath it:
desperately sketched lines of force
under this abhorrent cover.
I can no longer cut my fingernails,
and file the brittle claws to some more human shape,
but even so I sometimes scar myself as I scratch:
my arms look like I keep an angry cat.
My eyes used to sparkle, and now they seep,
proving my life a constant, low-level lamentation.
Day and night tears gather too cowardly to fall.
I had eyebrows once, didn't really notice them,
but now I have a horrible forest of hair
that stretches above my sockets

and shades them deeply: my eyes seem trapped
against the mica-backed wall of some dark cave.
　　When I look at you, it is the gaze of… what?
What beast or devil stares out of these holes?
　　It is a fearful thing to look at an old man:
you look at me and don't think that I am human,
that there's no link between the man I was
and the mumbling soft-mouthed thing I have become.


　　I pick up a book, or have one given me:
*Here you are, Homunculus, why not read a book?*
The letters blur and split in two,
and pages I recognise are larger in my hands.
My eyes are filled with clouds,
and every now and then a bright light behind them.
　　I think night has fallen by mid-afternoon:
isn't that the very definition of hell,
to live in eternal thick and thickening fog?


　　Which preacher or prophet screwed things up so badly,
told us to love our afflictions,
to ask for more of them, beg for corruption,
call for our bodies to suffer further, suffer faster?
The ascetics who tell us to pray for boils
are, to put it politely, nuts.


　　I am sick, and in sickness there is danger;
food brings me no joy: funeral baked meats.
All pleasure is the sick pleasure of a funeral.
We move from one state of unhappiness to another,
and lessen our lives, that we may continue to live:
cigarettes are extinct; alcohol is extinct.
*Every morning I wake up dreaming*
*I've got bad breath. My whole body's rotting…*

I used to eat everything: slick little snails, tripe and onions,
steak so bloody you could imagine a miracle:
that it might get up from your plate and walk.
   I would order shells and offal in restaurants:
liver and langoustines, whelk and small sheep's brains.
And now, if I have a relapse – *steak-frites, vin rouge* –
I know from the very first mouthful I'll regret it,
and so I abstain, and regret having abstained.
   When I was a baby, the doctor prescribed me Guinness:
what'd he say now if I asked for a pint?
I had a refined palate; now I mouth pap:
drool and food gather, dry where my lips meet:
pulped-down proteins crust in my wispy beard.
   My tongue forgets to work: I fill my mouth
and have to pause and think *what happens next?*
Old turtle mouth, jaw that hangs loose from my skull:
for my next trick, I'll try to eat a cough sweet,
sucking and slurping, then the final worrying *crack*.
~~Wine~~ | ~~women~~ | ~~song~~: a line scored through each word,
~~women~~ scored through twice, with unnecessary vigour.
They used to make life bearable, now they mock me:
*wine is a mocker*, but un-wine, non-wine, mocks harder.

   I am a cannibal on myself. Tick by tock,
nature chews itself down, dissolves and dribbles away.
   I am a knight, charging over and again into a mirror:
splinters of glass and lance cut me to shreds.
   I have tried patent remedies, antibiotics;
have burnt sage, sat in ashrams, been injected
with plasms I didn't ask about too closely,
and none of this has helped me in the slightest.
In the past, perhaps it would have done,
but when nature fails, art cannot be her substitute:
loss following on from loss

makes even the initial loss hard to bear.
I shit little pellets, like a rabbit,
and when I piss a whole teaspoonful
of sad yet virulently yellow urine,
I often, secretly, wheeze and punch the air.

My life is a Gothic cathedral, blocks of stone
with more stone leaning against it
to stop what stone wants to do, which is fall down.
A Gothic cathedral? Balls, my life is *Jenga*.
    Party game, place of worship, no difference:
whatever it is, my life is shuddering and in trouble,
and I shore these fragments against it,
which is useless.
Time comes and tears the temple down.
    *Now I got my way*
*Now I got my way*
*Now I got my way*
*And I'll tear this building down.*
    Samson sang that just before he died,
or was it the Big Bad Wolf?

    Maybe out there there's something
I could visit and enjoy?
An art gallery, a public hanging,
a football match, a play?
Anything that would let an old man cast a veil
over so, so many troubles and hurts?
    I will get dressed up and they will see me
and whisper, *mutton dressed as mutton.*
I will clean my face and they will see me
and say out loud, *doesn't he look tired?*
I will be, just be, exist and nothing more,
and they will wonder right in my ear:

*I thought he was dead? Shouldn't he be dead?*
    And then they will say, *Oh, alright for some,*
*coming out here, not a care on his mind,*
*some of us have jobs to go to in the morning.*
Or else, *How odd to see you out here, Homunculus,*
*I wouldn't have thought this was your kind of crowd.*
    Yes, even our pleasures are blamed now:
an old man in public is out of place,
unworthy, indecent, almost a little obscene.
    What's the point of having money
if you can't spend it? What's the point
of my having money if I can't spend it
without fingers being pointed,
and mutterings behind my back?
If you take away my pleasure,
what would you have me do?
Sit in rags on a heap of gold?
It's sinful to have earned a little nest-egg,
and equally sinful to want to spend it?
Is this my torment: to watch over my gold
and know that if I buy stuff I'll be damned?
    ...*Questions, questions*...
    Old age is the story of that man in the limpid pool,
bending down to quench his thirst
as the water sinks from his parched, begging lips.
    My job – others so kindly interpret it for me –
to be the guardian, not the master, of my wealth,
to hold in trust for others
that which I am assumed to no longer need.
    In this story I am the dragon,
winding round the gold-leafed trees,
hissing and showing the pink roof of my mouth
to anyone who comes to take the apples,
these golden apples which I do not eat.

In the middle of the night, I wake up:
My cares are gnawing me from the inside out.
    I hold onto what I can no longer acquire,
and though I lose nothing
I feel it run through my fingers like sand.


    An old man stands at a slight angle to the world,
is unsure of his footing, needs always to adjust
where he stands, and how he takes each step.
    He is a coward, back at school again,
remembering the bullied filth of his youth.
Flashback: his bedclothes torn to the ground
every day, his accent mocked, his boring life
chewed up and spat on. *What's that you're eating?*
*Smells like shit. What are you wearing?*
*You look like a cunt. Are you smiling?*
*Stop grinning like a fuckwit, you fuckwit.*
On one memorable occasion, his schoolmates –
nature lovers all – held him down to the ground
and waited for the housemaster's dog,
Max, to jizz excitedly up his leg.
    So, he's got history, all that's left to him,
and there are no holidays, and the whole world
is like his regretted, cruel and painful school.
    *...Made me the man I am today...*
    Homunculus cringes at what might happen to him,
what he has done (it always is his fault).
    And the flipside to this: the arrogance of age,
the absolute certainty, almost knowledge,
that things were better then than they are now,
that no amount of sanity will save the world
when the world is determined to run mad.
    If he thought about it, he might think it odd
that the only things still valuable

are the things he is expert in,
the only worthwhile info the info he's obtained.
But he doesn't think about it;
he's too grown up to think.
He has just enough wisdom
to take the final, clinching step into folly.
    *…Old man yells at cloud…*
    He is sunk deep into his anecdotage:
he has a list of stories ready to deploy
as soon as he can find a tiny conversational hook.
He's boring, because he repeats himself,
and even if they are clean, and, on occasion,
genuinely funny, his stories are hateful.
    At times he will realise this, fade out
in the middle of his telling, pretend his mind
has wandered, which is better than the truth:
he knows he is dull, and no one likes him.
But, still, it is impossible for him to believe
that other people possess imagination:
empathy burns off him like alcohol off a plum pudding.
Everyone in his mind is a zombie,
because that's how he is in his own mind.
    Or, his hearer will sometimes walk off,
and he will carry on talking: is the sound enough
to make him think he still has his strength,
even if his strength is only in his tongue?
    But it's not enough, nowhere near enough
to fill the air with noise like this:
he can caw as much as he likes, the old raven,
do his impression of an irate radio station.
    Nothing will ever be enough for him:
he rejects the things he used to love.
    And then, the bullied child come full circle,
he shows – good sport! – that he can laugh at himself,

unleashes his embarrassed, oh-so-English grin
in the centre of the jeering crowd.
Does he get it? Does he not get it? Does it matter?
He lets himself seem happy in his shame.

　　Here they come, the first signs of death;
here it is, life running out of us,
vitality dribbling down,
the last few drops of syrup in the jar.
　　Didn't they used to make offerings
of honey, syrup and other raw sweet things
at the tombs and shaded temples of their Gods?
　　Nothing about him is the same:
the face is different, the colour different,
the set of his feet, the walk, the shape are all different.
*Ce n'est plus la même personne.*
It is no longer the same person.
(Think on this, that *personne* in French
can also mean, does also mean, *nobody*.
'Who goes there?' '*Personne.*')
　　Our bodies change. I'm going to bring you in here,
and give you this bit in the first person plural:
this will happen to all of us, if we get this far.
　　Our bodies change. This robe we wear,
which once seemed too short, almost revealing,
now slips from our shoulders and dwarfs us.
Even our clothes are looming over us.
Belts need extra holes, skirts need to be taken in,
the flesh melts from our bones like wax.
　　And our bones melt too: our skeletons,
which we always thought the byword
for solidity and structure, shrink and shrivel.
It's astonishing, how small we get so fast.
*We shrink together, grow wonderfully smaller.*

An old man can no longer look up at the sky.
Backs are bent, and twisted, and pay
for years of desk-work, accounts and figures,
*those long tiny little columns in the* Wall Street Journal.
Old men can only look at the ground
whence they were born and to which they'll soon return.
Dark thoughts without the chance of grace:
*It's best you learn your fucking place.*

   *I will burn you to dust*
*and then I will burn the dust to air*
*and then I will burn the air into flowers that will not touch me*
*because they have their arms in the ground.*

   He'll fulfil the riddle, walk on three legs,
sometimes even on four, like a suckling child.
And sometimes he will fall and writhe in the mud.

Everything seeks at the end to go home,
to go back to the tit, to go back to the womb.
And everything now becomes nothing again,
as it had been before it once learnt to begin.

   (I don't want to bore you with words,
but think what hangs between these languages:
the French text gives us *néant*,
the constant expectation, the being-about-to-be-born;
Latin has *nihil*, which leads to *annihilation*,
the grinding into dust, the hopeless eternal void.
English is descriptive, *no-thing* opposes *some-thing*:
a hole is a place where nothing is.)

   Here is old age, slumped over his walking stick,
not walking, but slumped, afraid of collapse.

With an immense effort, he strikes the ground,
strikes it again and again though he knows it won't listen.
The hollow ground clonks and resonates,
and sends him his own blows and steps in mocking echo,
as if to say, *old man, I refute you thus!*
And, meanwhile, he seems to speak:
his wrinkled old mouth opens and shuts
like a barn door in a gale.
The day is calm: the gale's inside his head.

*Mother. Mother earth,*
*take pity on your son,*
*hold me to your breast*
*to keep my cold limbs warm.*

*The young avoid my gaze,*
*and hurry to escape me:*
*why do you let me live*
*when all the world hates me?*

*I owe the Gods no fee:*
*my days have run their course.*
*Allow my native soil*
*to take and keep my corpse.*

*Why let me bear my pain,*
*one sick day to another?*
*If you allow this shame,*
*you are not my mother.*

This said, feeling quite pleased with himself
to have created, *in extremis,* even such shonky verses,
he props himself on his essential stick
and totters off to his bed – straw and bugs,

uncomfortable and prickly, the living parallel
to the other mattress that will soon welcome him.

And when he lies down – you can see what's coming –
he looks like he will look when the cuckoo clock
springs for him: a pile of bones
formed into some vague armature,
unaware that the living clay will never more
be slapped on and shaped up to make a body,
unaware that he will never again be a man.
*On n'aperçoit, hélas! que les os d'un corps exténué.*
I spend more time than ever in bed,
a kind of preparation, lying and lying flat.
The more I lie, the more lying becomes my life,
and is – the obvious question – *is* this life?
To curl like an animal seeking warmth?
Even a bed is not the refuge it once was.
Living itself, the sensitivity dials turned up
to eleven, is more a torment than not.
A bright warm day: sun-cream, factor 50+,
and a hat, and long sleeves, and still you burn.
Gentle clouds cover the sun: scarf and a thick coat,
shivering as the thermometer hits fifteen degrees.
Rain. Oh, allow me to vanish in eternal rain!
But rain turns the house into a prison:
you look out of windows at nothing but weather,
weather you once would have genekelleyed through,
standing under waterspouts, singing and dancing.
If it is cold, you will never be warm again:
for the old man, cold weather starts in the heart,
frozen blood forced round an ever-chilling body.
Even dew – fucking *dew*! – makes us think twice:
what if it soaks our shoes, what if we get cold feet?
A chill could very easily

mount to our chest and kill us.
Spring: lambs and daffodils, potential death.
Autumn: russet leaves and apples, potential death.
    You have to live like the world is out to get you,
and – let me tell you something – it is.


    I'm particularly worried about this cough.


    I know… *moan moan moan*… but do I really exist
when such things as e.g. air and light
are no longer simple benefits
but grow heavy and almost unwelcome?
    The rasp of oxygen hitting your alveoli,
as though the air could think, and rebel:
*what have you done to deserve me?*
    When you draw back the curtains
another perfect bright day makes you squint
and feel ever-so-slightly sick.


    Even sleep, sweet rest, once so pleasant,
decides that it can give your couch a miss,
or else comes late, grudging or perfunctory:
*I'll give you half an hour now,*
*then an hour just before daybreak,*
*that's all I can spare. Quit whining.*
    And that tiny modicum is ruffled and harassed
by dreams you almost dare not repeat.
Not the bright surrealism of youth,
when dreams were mostly fun, boring anecdotes,
but the true dreams of old age, premonitions
of the inevitable future, or new translations
of the classics: the dream of falling
hits you far more often than the dream of flying.

When I was young, I would often wake myself
by laughing, and lie in the dark infused
by an inchoate sense of warm joy.
Let me tell you, buddy, those days are gone.

  The bed seemed soft when you lay down,
but now is an airless, breathless, spiny desert.
No need to wander in the wilderness
when the wilderness comes for you at night.
I took a thinner blanket than usual:
it is still oppressive, heavy as a tombstone.
  I get up from bed in the middle of the night,
for the usual reasons, yes, but also for the terror,
the sheer black regular alarm clock terror,
the fear of what will happen
that is a part itself of what will happen.
*A penny saved is a penny earned.*
*A trouble shared is a trouble halved.*
*A fear anticipated is a double fear...*
My heart beats harsh and hard when I wake,
trapped under the rubble of my body,
desperate for someone to set it free.
  The constant war – me vs. my prospective corpse –
is entering an endgame. There will be no victory.
The parts I felt might hold out the longest
were the first to fall, resigned, to the new order.
Limbs were quislings, mind has also collaborated;
fraternising with the enemy is painful.
  When we have fought ourselves into the ground
death will be there like Caesar to kill the survivors.
  I feel unknown things crack within me
and my regret is that the frontline sawbones
will not stop struggling – damn the Hippocratic oath! –
to send me out each morning weaker to the fight.

I am wearing a coat of evil.
A rucksack of evil on my back, and strapped to that
a lifetime's supply of evil, pain and doubt.
    I look like a wandering mushroom, a refugee
who just had time to gather everything bad
before the soldiers came, or the tide came in.
    Mortification of the flesh, a teachable moment:
I am weighted down with this shit
so I may learn to live weighted down.
Who wants this to last any longer than it does?
Who wants to be able to watch himself –
step by step, indignity by indignity –
fade and fail and fight and inevitably lose?
*Qui voudrait se voir dépérir et mourir par degrés?*
It is best to give in; it is best to give up;
it is best to allow death a single, straightforward victory
rather than hang around, opening the door
a little wider every day, making room for a bony foot.
    When death and life are mingled,
it's embarrassing for everybody:
death snaps and snarls at a victory
that is deferred just to the point of annoyance;
life weakens, refuses to accept that it has lost.
A pub bore, the argument over, buttonholes,
pint in hand, to say *and another thing…*
when all anyone wants to do is play darts.

    Mind and body, both of them cut clean off,
perfect like the last scene of *The Sopranos*.

    That would be the ideal.

    You're going to laugh, but I don't complain that much.
I don't complain that this is happening to me:

it would be wrong to fight against the laws of nature.
A bull, randy and red-sparked, will grow weak with age;
a fine racehorse will lose its line, its beauty;
a lion observes how, while it once was angry,
with roars and tail-lashes *pá parar un tren*,
all it wants now is to curl up by the fire and purr.
The tiger walks slowly by the shore of the Caspian Sea.
Even rocks, even mountains, are beaten down by time:
this pebble was once a boulder.
    Time is like a bear, licking all things to form them,
licking enthusiastically, licking them down to nothing.
I cannot think of a single object that survives time.

    And I would like to avoid all this,
get things over and done with:
if I know that horrors are going to come,
why wait and deal with them individually?
Better to prevent the shame you know,
the shame that is coming round the hill
and whistling death as it comes;
better to leap with your eyes open
than live fear for as long as your body permits it.

    And, one thing is certain, it can always get worse:
even totting it up on bent and arthritic fingers
you always miss something from the kill list.
I'm not saying it lacks variety:
if you could look at it from the outside
there might be interest in the observation,
how every single part of you can fail.
But I am in this cage, and cannot even sing.

    And it won't just be me who's failing,
or, rather, my failure will corrupt

a whole network of relations and duties.
Deadly pragmatism – *we need to be prepared*
*for what comes after... you know... when he...* –
will break forth into arguments
and mistrust and violence.
The squabbles, a dogfight for the best china
and the keys to the country estate.
I will become a thing transformed
into net worth and probate:
not one friend will remain to comfort me
without an eye on the main chance.

    Boys and girls no longer call me *sir*.
They have their reasons, their justifications,
but basically they're just embarrassed
to waste respect on one who'll soon be dead,
who cannot give them material help.
    They mock me, limp alongside
in a cruel accurate parody of my walk.
They stutter like me, spit when they talk,
nod their head just like I nod mine.
And yes, this will happen to them too;
they will decay as I have decayed,
but that's a long-term consolation
for a current and creeping annoyance.
    *...I'm not crying in the wilderness;*
*You're crying in the wilderness...*
    My eyes may be weak, but the residue
of sense in them processes this sight:
I see the children's mimicry,
and seeing them mock me and what I feel
mocks me makes me feel doubly mocked.
    *...Torture and torment...*

Call that man happy who has lived his life
calmly and tranquil to a gentle end.

IT IS HARSH FOR UNHAPPY PEOPLE TO REMEMBER
THAT THEY ONCE WERE HAPPY. IF ONE HAS FALLEN
FROM HAPPINESS, THE FALL ITSELF IS UNBEARABLE.

My battery is low and it's getting dark.

## II.

By convention, we will give her a false name.
I will call her Liquorice, for she is dark but comely
and lots of my friends don't like her.
    But I like her, and that's what matters:
for a long time I wanted nothing more
than to breathe the same air as her,
to turn orgasm, appetite, to the focus of a life.
    We've been together for years, and many days
have been lost within the small walls
of our small-walled flat, scorning the world
when the only world we wanted was with us, there.
    I would lie back, my erect member a gnomon;
time would pass by in a mess of shadows and sperm.
Or she would lean over and, ever so gently,
take my life into her hands.
    There were moments when I could overcome myself:
my pouchy face, my spongy gut, and be…
if not pure, then at least, for a moment, sacred.
Yes, there was religion in how we loved:
to begin with I couldn't believe we were there,
but she told me to place my doubtful finger
to the wound between her thighs.
    Days passed in joy, and I didn't notice
how with the years love, love has passed as well.

    I try to embrace her and she shrugs me off.
I try to kiss her and she turns the other cheek.
*What is it?* I ask, and am scared what her answer will be.

She doesn't want me anymore.
She wants new men and younger loves.
She wants to walk with a new lover,
mazy with sex, in a public park.
   She says I am old and ugly and falling apart,
which is true, but doesn't this body contain
the memories of how we started out?
Every inch of my grazed anatomy is hers,
has been hers, affected by her.
   Can't she care even for our first meeting,
that muggy afternoon – *is that a rainbow?* –
when we took to bed for the first time,
discovered how to take pleasure from one another?
(A few final thrusts, then silence and stasis
and everything covered in our shared sweet sweat.
I sweated so much I thought I was crying.)
   *No, my memory of that day,* she said,
*lasted only till your smell faded from my fingers.*


   But if I've grown old, I've grown old with her,
and isn't old age something we've worked on together?
Ungrateful and faithless, she says *no,*
and thinks up reasons why this is my fault.


   Apparently, she was out with a friend,
and saw me passing by the café where they sat,
and something clicked. She didn't knock on the glass
to get my attention, didn't wave or stand up.
   A reflex took her, and she turned away,
pretended to look for something in her handbag.
And then, when she sat up – lip-salve, apparently –
she said this without thinking, almost in a trance:
   *Can you believe I loved that man?*
   *Can you believe he loved me back?*

*I mean, can you believe it?*
*We practically lived in bed together.*
*Can you believe I went down on his mushroom dick?*
　　And then she retched, wretched
(another reflex, reflux),
and had to run to the restroom to throw up.
　　All our love she threw up, hacking up Eros
and years of comfort and affection,
and when she came back to the table –
*Did you pay already? Have you got any gum?* –
she had nothing for me but curses and imprecations.


　　Is this the way old age is paying me back?
Paying me back for what? What did I do?
It's as though it were shameful
to acknowledge the tenderness I once inspired.
　　Would it be better for me to have spent my time alone,
like Simeon Stylites up his pillar, lonely but safe,
not suffering any hurt and hurting no one,
than to come down to the world,
bruised and radiant, and find myself now
the subject of insults I may or may not deserve?
　　You don't love people, you invent them.
Time has broken everything down,
and still it marches on.


　　As for Liquorice, she has a few grey hairs –
the backs of her hands are foxed like an old book –
but she is still beautiful – *trop belle* –
and knows that she has held herself together
all the time that I was breaking and fading.
The Homunculus years she gives up as a bad job,
thirty years in the same house, a lifetime, gone.

She has kept herself in shape, taken every course
that offered – by stretching or swimming,
by breathing or running or bending or starving –
the forever-distant prospect of eternal youth.
    In profile she could pass for twenty-five
(though each year swings her in orbit
a little further from that magic quarter-century).
    But I don't want to bitch about her:
she is still beautiful, a dog's tail liveliness in her.
    She came to my life like a purifying flame,
and burnt everything down, herself included,
and as I pick through the white ash
of my self-respect, and of our years together,
there are still dangerous points
where her beauty flares once again, and dazzles.
    An argument in favour of generous time,
time whom I hate, who seems always to knock
my most precious ornaments to the floor –
even you, clumsy time, make the effort
to save some trinkets from being crushed or broken.
Not everything has to die, not entirely.

*But did this flesh mean it all to you?*
*Were you beholden to this flesh?*
*Was this flesh what you only loved?*
*For this flesh will be gone, and you will*
*see it go and gone. If you are lucky.*

Young men have their memories to keep them warm,
the inexhaustible blanket of their memories:
home-grown erotica, or just more innocent stuff –
the afternoon when you and she first discovered
the city together, alleys you saw once only,
the comically bitter coffee as you hid from the rain,

and then, again, the sun – *is that a rainbow?* –
as you pondered whether or not to take her hand.
No matter how appalling the present might be,
the past can be glorious, unclouded, and happy.
I stand and scream silently into the mirror.

My arms are weak, my legs tremble,
and were I to embrace her
it would be a parody of our past embraces;
I cannot hold her, hold her back.
    It is misery alone that clings to me.
I run through the list of what I had,
and cross off every item.

Nothing remains for me but the present,
and I've already gone into detail about that,
how it's all failing, foundering;
I am the captain of a breached ship
and it's *when* rather than *if* the final, lifeboat-less
head-over-heels up-tip will happen
and we will slide under, streamlined, downwards.

Liquorice, am I an animal? Will there be nothing
left of me when I close my eyes?
*I sometimes imagined my life without me:*
*when I died, the whole world would die with me,*
*grey clouds over empty plazas,*
*deer and bird-shit reclaiming the roads.*
    But we are creatures of habit, we creatures.
Think of this, Liquorice, an argument taken from nature:
all animals have their happy lands,
and will run back to the places they have known.
    This is a counsel of desperation –
I know this even before I start to speak.

I don't know if you've thought about this,
but think about the cows on the common ground –
you always see their version of pastoral
ranged in the same pattern under the same trees.
Poor little lambs that have lost their way,
little black sheep that have gone astray,
ask to be shown the way to go home.
  And the bird of bards, the nightingale,
sings happier in its accustomed bush.
(There's a joke here about my accustomed bush,
but I won't be the one to make it…)
  Even the wildest of beasts has its own
hollow or burrow, dray or sett to return to,
and you, Liquorice, are hell-bent on leaving
a home that has been safe to you, and loving,
for what? An unknown future.
  Isn't it better to stick to what you know,
things that have been shown to be trustworthy?
Newness always brings a thousand doubtful chances.


  Look, I'm old, but your hair grows white as mine is:
doesn't it make sense for us to stay together?
If I am, yes, decrepit, ruined, impotent,
can't you remember that I wasn't always so:
can't it make you happy that I made you happy –
*was that a rainbow once?* – is that a line that works?
  You don't think a man dies when he retires, do you?
Remember the winemaker we both know,
old, shivering by the hearth, a glass of *marc* every evening:
he replanted, singlehanded, the three hills
by his bodega, squeezed his fruit
into this thick and tongue-coating wine.
Will we ignore his years of useful labour
because today he's pickled, cold and useless?

Old soldiers can't return to their old wars,
but when they fought they changed the world.
　　Animals again, for I am no more than an animal:
we put our livestock out to pasture
when it can no longer serve us –
it's not a question – I hope it's not a question –
of *Good horse, Titus… time to fetch the air-gun.*
I was not born to be boiled for glue.
　　And I am not so useless:
I write as well as I once did,
and make you the subject of all my poems.


　　Come on, Liquorice, how about it?
Is old age nothing, is it worth no respect?
You want to live a long life, just as I do,
and would you dare condemn the thing you want?
Who wishes to walk a long path,
then sets that path around with blocks and difficulties?
　　Surely we should look for what ease we can,
and seek it together.


　　Oh, if you cannot think of me
as a friend, or a brother;
if you cannot think of me as a lover;
call me something at least,
call me *batiushka, little father,*
someone who can live with you,
advise you,
who loves you.


　　Let our love die out, if it must die out.
But don't turn your face away from me in pride
when you have it in your hands
to be merciful.

Not love, mercy.

Reason will always triumph over blind strength.
This must be true. I'll force it to be true.

I've cried enough,
as much as I'm allowed to cry,
about my old age;
it is cruel
to halt so long at the grave of these memories.

III.


Today, I'm speaking in tongues.
   Instead of the voice of some God
demanding obeisance, obedience and/or vengeance,
I come out with *jinkies!*, *zoinks!* and a loud *ruh-roh!*
   Yes, the wobbly screen is in place,
and we are scoobydooing back to the past.
Here we are now, fifty-five years ago,
with a mystery to solve.


   Whiskey, I called her, for her sharpness on the tongue.
Long S, I called her, for how her body curved and bent.


   *Let's split up and look for clues!*


   It was in Chicago, America's second city,
renowned back then for its fecundity:
Long S and I met, and got on like Grenfell Tower.


   Don't worry, by the way, this story won't have a moral:
it's more a breathing space in my catalogue of death.


   *I was in love with you, Whiskey,*
*I was almost driven mad:*
*so much in love with you, Whiskey,*
*it made me pale and sad.*


   I had never been in love before,
and this was love and sex and desire,

all wrapped up with a bow around it.
    I was more worried about my inexperience,
wandering through the grad-school world like Candide,
handsome, twenty-two years old.
    *…the best of all possible worlds…*

    And she felt the same, the same arrow
to her similar-sized and palpitating heart.
    She wandered round her flat,
which suddenly seemed too small for what she was.
She needed a city to explode into.

    We would meet all days in secret,
and fail to satisfy our desires.
Or rather, constantly satisfy our desires,
only to realise that what we did
was push the boundaries of our desire back further.
    Now I think of it, the best moments have been like this:
a child, screen-struck in a cinema,
watching life unfurl into his eyes.
    Bad analogy, for when we got to the cinema,
we had no eyes for the movie;
no eyes at all, only mouths and silent, frantic hands.

    *What does illicit frotting of the clitoris elicit?*

    *Is carnal knowledge the knowledge*
    *that comes from research or from revelation?*

    Or else, she would send me letters of assignation –
remember those? Remember letters at all? –
*I will be alone outside the public library.*
*Wednesday, 10 a.m. I have gin and it will be raining.*
And gin and rainwater would be our cocktail.

So, pretty perfect, right?
No, hence the secrecy.

*Was it the creepy old funfair owner?*

No. Whiskey's Mother. Whiskey was rich,
and I was not. And I was arrogant,
and cocksure, and painted all colours
of unspecified post-adolescent pathetic.
So, Mother was right to be suspicious.
She kept Long S on a chain, Whiskey in her cask.
Mother was not difficult to trick –
afternoons in hotels I couldn't afford,
or shared flats when I'd sent my roommates packing,
the many chances we got for consequential intercourse,
all this was proof of that –
but if we had been open, ever,
had ever stood up to her and openly declared our love,
I would have been burnt alive,
and Whiskey would have been locked away.

And Mother was astute, protean:
she monitored her daughter's dates with girlfriends,
cinema trips, extracurricular activities,
forcing Long S into elaborate and exhausting lies,
which almost worked, or worked for a time.

But there's only so long you can hide yourself,
and every time our paths crossed,
I could see the old spider putting two and two together.
    (Meanwhile, we took all chances we could
to carry on putting one and one together.)
    The last week or so was spiced with danger,
including one stupid occasion

when I almost met Mother
coming up the fire escape as I was coming down.
   *… As if I could escape this fire…*

And then, disaster, a bad star in the heavens.

We were discovered, I can't remember how,
or yes, it comes back to me, our tight guard slipped,
a willed discrepancy in the network of lies:
   *I thought you were going to that gallery with Velma,*
*but then I rang Velma's mother,*
*and she said… but you said…*
love came out into the open, and started to rust.

But not at once. In her desire to part us,
all Mother did was drive us closer together:
her blows and scolding a kind of spider-glue,
wrapping us as one, allied against her.
   Blowing on the fire as though it were a candle
sent our embers to new, dry kindling:
her opposition was fuel and not cool water.
   It was a new kind of love, very sudden,
where responsibility loomed
in land that had been irresponsible.
My first thought: *I will deal with this.*

Long S came round to my flat that evening,
shooed me away from the kitchen table
and the night-time vodka and chatter.
   I said goodbye to my friends –
the Philosopher, the Creepy Funfair Owner –
and followed her into the back room,
almost windowless, a mattress on the floor,
for which I had the privilege

of paying two-thirds of my monthly stipend.
    *... I lived back then on noodles and Whiskey...*

*Here, look at me,* she said, and undid her dress,
not as a prelude to love, but as the thing itself:
one of the sleeves was torn, and her pure back,
over which I had leant so often,
was now a new text of scratches and marks,
glyphs and wedges of a language I did not know,
but which I could with ease interpret.
    Even so, she talked me through it:
this was the mark of her Mother's fingernails,
this here where she had slapped her, left and right.
The long mark, purple now fading to blue,
was one good blow she'd got in with the poker.

*All this is for you,* as I fetched the embrocation,
*I would take this, and worse, a thousand times,
all this for you. The price I pay for you.
I knew you loved me as the blows came down.*
    I laid her down, and rubbed the wounds,
and she started to drift off to sleep.
*It's worth it if you love me,* she muttered,
her eyes closed, her Whiskey mouth at my ear.
*There's no love without some suffering.*

    I lay with her in the dark,
neon light flicking at the tiny curtain-less window
and was in love, and afraid,
and didn't know what to do.

    She had one arm across my chest,
and wriggled in her sleep, her thigh
between my thighs.

I could feel her belly, ever so slightly swollen,
press warm against my belly and my groin.
Getting away was a tricky operation,
and she made a soft protesting noise
as I lifted her arm up, shifted off the mattress.
    But when I was free,
I stood up silently, and watched her,
as she slept, naked and bruised, under the neon.
    My thoughts were lost
in that odd time after any key event,
before you turn your troubles into a story.
    I walked silently through to the kitchen,
careful to shut the bedroom door behind me.


    *What's up?* the Philosopher asked, and then,
because philosophy cannot always console us,
he poured me a tumblerful of vodka.
    I drank it down and said nothing,
and drank the second and said nothing,
and then was ready to speak,
and sat back,
and spoke.


    *It's Whiskey. I need your help, Philosopher.*
*You've seen us together, and you've seen me*
*alone, wondering what to do.*
*And I need your help. Can you help?*
    And he looked puzzled, poured a little more vodka,
just a capful, into my empty tumbler.
    I watched the viscous, almost frozen liquid
climb the sides of the glass on thick legs, and fall.
    *I'll try to help, but you need*
*to be a little more specific, Homunculus.*
*What is it? What's gone wrong?*

*I can't help you if I can't define your sickness:*
*if you can't even say what's up with you*
*then what use can I be?*
*Come on, let it out, pierce the boil.*

I was shy of speaking, a little drunk,
scared to put my real fear –
that maybe slightly swollen belly – into words.
  The Philosopher shifted his chair
until he was sitting next to me,
then put his arm round my shoulders
and whispered. *Just tell me what's up,*
*come on, ¡ánimo! a problem shared*
*is a problem halved, a fear anticipated*
*is a smaller fear… You're not in any trouble…*

  I fell off my chair: the vodka and my worries
hit me both at once, and I cried thick vodka tears.
And through these pathetic tears I spoke to him,
and told him everything, all I have only hinted at.

  *Well, why not marry her?* the Philosopher said.
  *Would that solve anything?* I replied.
  He burst out laughing, as philosophers often do
when faced with a real world that seems ridiculous.

  *Look, the world is made of experiences,*
*and then memories*
*and interpretations,*
*which are also experiences,*
*further experience bred from former experience.*

*It's all a mishmash of actual events and the spin we put on them, so*
*no, getting married wouldn't change that much.*

*The world you live in would still be made half of memory and half
of actual fact.*

*The principle of all love is memory.*

*On the other hand, I'm speaking as a philosopher, and for people
who don't think like me a wedding ring is a pretty good way of
solving the world.*

    Or look at it like this, my drunk mind said to me,
*Love is happy to receive these blows.*
I had, the next morning,
a hangover that made my teeth hurt.

    The Philosopher interceded with Whiskey's parents.
He got professors to call and sing my praises:
the great future that I imagined half a joke
became, in their telling, something solid and certain.
    *Your Homunculus is a safe bet for the future*
was reported to me as something someone said –
academics careful not to put it in writing.
(*Why do you take notes? Lawyers don't take notes.*)
    Little by little, the whole university system
won round these two wealthy and protective parents.

    *Now let's see who the Headless Assman really is!*

    This was the next stage of my Whiskey love:
condoned, connived at, chaperoned:
I went to ballgames with her father,
allowed him to explain the rules to me
every single time – they never sank in.
I had vast uncomfortable meals with her family,
sitting, slightly shell-shocked, holding Whiskey's hand.

Cousins came out of the woodwork to congratulate me,
and what was now permitted
became dull and undesired.
  Nothing cools the heart
like your in-laws' approval.


  Whiskey, the bruises healed,
her heart healed too, left me.


  And when we had had the talk, and she had left,
taking with her a book or two she said were hers
and a shirt of mine she had once worn
over her naked body,
I felt – I have to admit it – relieved.
Had I been unhappy all this while?


  *Better not to get involved,*
*better to stand too far back*
*than love too close, and suffer.*
  This was my conscience speaking to me,
my so-called good angel –
I must have been really gone.


  The Philosopher heard what had happened,
as he heard everything, with equanimity.
  *Well, that love's gone, crushed and fallen –*
*you've been crushed and fallen, but you're learning.*
  *You can stand up straight and say*
*with a straight face, that you have beaten*
*love and desire and wisdom too:*
*faced up to them all and beaten them.*

Being given free rein to sin removed my desire to sin.
I left soon after and never returned.

I sometimes think about Long S's swollen belly,
what it might have meant, how I could return one day
and wander the streets, maybe sit in a café
and be surprised and happy
to watch my by-blow
blow by.

I was never even in Chicago,
though I would say that, wouldn't I?

*And I would have gotten away with it*

*Meddling kids*

IV.

How are you holding up?
There's still a way to go, stories of shame
that has now fermented into laughter.
History repeating itself as farce, farce, farce.
    Poetry makes nothing happen, perhaps,
but it's unarguable that poetry itself
is nothing, a way to fill time,
nothing at all when compared to a playground,
a military campaign, or even a cow-byre.
    Idle nothingness is what I want now:
it's just enough to watch the seasons change
for us to forget that years are passing –
such shifts and twitches fool us
and sometimes we like to be fooled.


    But some things are constant:
there was a girl… I'm running out
of false names to protect the innocent.
    She was white-skinned, and looked soft as an eider duck:
I'll call her Eider, because Blanche is boring.
    She was very beautiful, with clear brown eyes
she emphasised with careful make-up.
    She was a dancer; I saw her dancing
in a strange costume hemmed with bells and little cymbals,
and as she moved she made all kinds of sound:
the shimmer of her haunches, the ring of her hands.
    And after she had danced, she played the guitar
in artless accompaniment to another dancer,
and, after that, she played a song and sang alone.

I couldn't look at this new girl,
but instead saw how Eider's white-skinned fingers
deliberately drew out music.
    And – to prolong this vision into metaphor –
the music, and her playing, and her white-skinned fingers,
drew out from me the old familiar tune,
and suddenly I knew I was in love.


    Before we go any further, know this:
it never went any further than this.
My pure devotion to images in my mind,
to the thoughts of what love might be,
were the closest I came to any physical love.
    (If that means you want to skip this bit,
then – pervert! – of course I understand you.)


    Inside me, I had a picture of her face –
clearer than any photograph, that image behind my eyes –
and, Cubist-fashion, I broke her down:
features that flashed into my waking dreams.
    Her eyes I've mentioned, but alongside the eyes,
her mouth disarmed me, taut with concentration,
and sometimes, as she played the guitar,
the tip of a soft pink tongue had touched her lips
as she considered where to put her fingers next.
I spent whole nights in contemplation of that tongue.
    That single evening became a vast cosmology,
as I built and invented memories for us two.
I never stalked her, never really saw her again,
but I noted her real name,
and scribbled it on my workbooks,
like any child would, in his age of crushes.
    Imagine that: an older, apparently wiser man,
performing the charms and rituals of first love.

I had to keep control of myself.
I mean, I wasn't imagining a situation
in which, no sooner clap I eyes on her,
raucous gouts of claggy semen
schlep across the room to lewinsky her dress,
but one must be careful.

She lived with me; her image lived with me,
and all I had to do was close my eyes
to feel the joy of being with her,
as though she were next to me.
    I would talk to myself at inappropriate times –
a naïve dialogue that would break into song
as though I were a teapot in a Disney movie,
though the song I sang was only ever
the same song she had sung, that perfect night.
    Only a part of the song, a single brief snatch
from the main theme… I imitated to perfection
that moment when she had paused
and sought the notes she needed,
before dropping, triumphant and relieved,
onto a serviceable, approximate chord.
    No mockery in this: I fell so hard
that even her mistakes to me were perfect.

    *Mad, they told me I was mad!*
And maybe they were right –
there was Frankenstein's glint in my eye
as I pieced this love together from scraps of nothing.
*It's alive!* I muttered to myself
as I threw the switch and let the lightning down.

    This was not a love I was able to hide:
any friend of mine, who knew what I was like,

would have had it out of me in a moment:
*Homunculus, nice song… Who's the girl?*
It's hard to hide love, the fires of your heart
take and blacken everything they touch.
    The fire rises beneath your skin,
or else sinks away from it so rapidly,
that your blushing or pallor speaks
louder than any words would have done.

    And – here's the funny bit –
my dreams gave me away as well.
    Daydreams, fine: I could spend hours
in comfortable reverie and know that I was safe.
My daydream life was a parallel life:
eyes and mouth and sweet clumsy fingers
happening in my mind as I typed or taught my lessons.
    When it came to real sleep, my mind betrayed me,
my tongue spoke my dreams as though they were fact.
    *Eider!* I called out (using her real name,
because I only hide the truth from you).
    *Eider! Soft and willing, come here now!*
*Eider, why are you so slow?*
*The night is nearly over, and the day,*
*bright enemy of lovers…*

    Trouble was, I was having my siesta
in a public park, in the boho part of town,
and Eider's father, brothers and three strapping cousins
had used their shore leave to come and watch her dance.

    The old man heard me call her name,
as I lay within earshot of their picnic blanket:
he jumped up – *Oi, lads! Can you hear that?* –
and waited to hear his daughter's name again.

It came; he looked around, sure that he'd see her,
and saw me instead, my belly rising and falling,
my mind elsewhere, with a very obvious hard-on.

*You hear this?*
                    *Why's this guy saying Eider's name?*
*What's going on?*
                    *Who's he?*
                                    *Is he asleep?*
*What's that in his pocket?*

In this, and similar terms, they discussed my dream,
my spoken dream, my disrespect,
and wondered what to do next.

   *Let's see what he's got to say for himself...*

They woke me with a couple of gentle kicks,
and I blinked and stammered
and rushed back to myself,
to find myself surrounded by a fistful of Popeyes,
their sleeves rolled up to show off their tattoos.
   It was a tricky situation to get out of:
quick-talking only got me so far,
and I ended up standing them drinks all night
at Eider's nightclub, and I never talked to her.

I used to be held in some respect,
but they made sure to spread the story:
the older man, giddy as a schoolboy,
can't even keep his dreams to himself.
   Now it's made it as far as my local –
*afternoon, Homunculus, had any dreams?* –
my life turned to nicknames and double entendre.

(Actually, a *double* entendre would be welcome:
it's mostly unsubtle smut they throw at me:
*Dreaming Boy there, jerking off in his corner...*)

My sad life is empty of love,
even my imaginative sins are forbidden me.
I am shunned by both pleasure and vice –
pleasure in particular seems upset with me –
and I wish I had done what I only dreamed about.

But that's how it is: I can think back
to this embarrassing stepping-stone
on the way to being truly old,
when I moaned embarrassingly after a dancer.
But who can sound the mysteries of human nature,
explain why a normally sensible man
should behave so stupidly?

Vice seizes hold of us and drags us on,
and our blind hearts run after
what is always too far and further away.

v.

I was sent to the edge of our failing empire
on a mission that – at the time – seemed successful.
    In retrospect all diplomacy is useless.
    Everything nowadays is a staving-off,
a delay to the inevitable collapse
that we can minimise, soften a little,
but will always make itself shown in death.
(A stupid, commentary-on-itself world,
as though someone, caught in an avalanche,
would get out his phone and Google 'avalanches'.)
    I didn't realise this back then, took my job seriously,
and tried to broker an acceptable deal
between two parties, both of whom were liars.
    And as I worked on this treaty,
that seemed so important then
and in memory was clearly just waste-paper,
I let my defences fall and fell
into similar battles for my much-abusèd heart.
    She was with the delegation;
part of her first approach was clearly politics.
    I could riff here about how love is politics,
how sex is politics, how every human meeting
is at its root only politics –
not often have I seen this shown so bluntly.

    In retrospect all diplomacy is useless:
in retrospect she pretended to fall for me –
what really happened was I lost my head
and thought, as men so often do,

that I had at sixty
all the charms I'd had at seventeen.
    She was with the delegation,
and was assigned me as a cultural aide.
Her job to show me museums, restaurants,
the pleasant side of her ancient culture.
    We saw the holy rocks
that proved, she said, her country's claim on ours;
I argued with her, showed her the old cuneiform,
more glyphs and wedges – our clay language –
that proved, I said, our country's claim on hers.
    *Oh let's not argue*, she said with a laugh,
*you're here to sort all this out, aren't you?*
And I laughed as well, and said that I would try.
    We saw the art of their nineteenth-century masters,
the kinds of painting you can buy in any auction,
domestic scenes to purchase by the yard.
I said, *how nice*, and she said, mock offended,
*How nice? This knocks your Hockney into a cock-a-hoop!*
    So we laughed a little bit about my language,
and I thought how sweet her accent was:
the voice of someone clever,
putting thoughts into words you understand
in a language not quite her own
has always won me over, blindsided me.
    I was like Ulysses on his boat,
and this language came bouncing –
the Sirens speaking my own tongue –
I could not avoid its power, and let it bear me
overwhelmed, headfirst, to hidden reefs and shoals.

    That evening in the hard-currency restaurant –
smoking-hot lamb shashliks, hot sauce,
the hot wine in cast clay bottles –

she took my hand,
across the starched, offensive tablecloth,
and looked at me and said *Come on! Let's dance!*
    And I demurred, but then stood with her,
jogging from foot to foot in the classical postures
of pathetic embarrassed masculinity,
as the folk orchestra kicked off
and she swayed to its doleful rhythms.
    *Between the stolid pillars of the hall,*
*she danced, lithe and slender,*
*not so much lovely as alien.*
*She moved slow: the pleasure she promised*
*was secret and powerful as death.*
    Somehow the dance floor cleared:
she was there alone, dancing for me alone.
I remember most clearly how her curled hair
shook as she stamped her feet,
fell free and bounded against her soft white neck.


    We ended up in my hotel room,
both of us a little tipsy,
both of us perhaps pretending
to be a little tipsier than we were.
    But not just tipsy, I grew drunk
to uncover her breasts –
they fitted soft to the palm of my hand,
one hand covered one whole breast;
her nipples stood clear,
and tautened as I breathed on them.
    And then, demurely unclothed,
she sat on the side of the bed
and the line between her thighs,
and the line where her thighs met
her soft little stomach…

I could tell you about this,
but then I'd have to kill you.
　　All I can tell you
is that it killed me.


　　Oh, what drunkenness, what physical drunkenness,
to grasp her in my arms and hold her!
I squeezed her so close
her bones seemed to complain,
and I was just about to bring myself into her
when, *Oh stop please stop*, she cried out.
*Your arms are too strong and they hold me too tight;*
*my legs cannot support your body.*
　　Too late to rearrange, I withdrew,
and splashed her knee with a watery cum
like whey risen from milk, or lumpy spindrift.
　　My penis shrank in embarrassment
and I was suddenly stone cold sober.
　　In this moment of high disgrace,
as she walked away like a queen
to fetch some paper and dab her leg dry,
I suddenly realised how much this mattered,
how strongly I had decided I loved her
(yes, love, even that, after one afternoon
and a wispy, premature ejaculation).
I knew myself caught
and felt myself happy to be caught.
　　Homunculus is a simple man,
perhaps unsuited for bedroom diplomacy,
and she was from an ancient culture
with some, sustainable, claim on my own:
no surprise that I should be so well enticed,
that her charms and *bienséances*
should have wrapped my brain in silk.

Even King Arthur was defeated, even Merlin,
so what hope could I have
against such decorous treachery?
   From this moment, I ceased to be a diplomat,
I forgot about treaties and trade deals,
the delicate boundaries and balances,
backstops, lines on maps.
   I was a lover, a failed lover:
that was my identity and I lived it complete.

   *Go there!* says love, and I go.
*Sit here!* says love, and I sit.
*Stay!* says love. *Roll over! Beg!*

   A lover is from a more distinguished lineage
than any diplomat: even the Gods have loved.
(This is a short way of saying:
*even the Gods have humiliated themselves.*)

   She walked back from the bathroom,
a dead, glistening smear on her right knee.
Her knees were beautiful.
   She sat down next to me on the bed
where I lay, still in embarrassed shock,
too embarrassed and shocked even to lie
and murmur the traditional words:
*I'm sorry, this has never happened before...*
   She looked me in the face, and smiled:
*Poor Homunculus! Come here.*
She stretched herself beside me
and I felt her long heat,
breast to breast, belly to belly,
the warmth of her groin against me.
   We kissed, and rested,

and I slowly forgot my shame.

Our second time was successful,
and the third, and – God help me! – the fourth.
    Dawn came into the hotel room,
through the orange viscose curtains,
casting orange light on all our naked flesh
(in such light, every shade of skin's unnatural,
from presidential lobster to Benidorm paedophile),
then she rolled away from me,
got up, showered, dressed, and left.
    I stayed in bed, happy and empty,
empty and happy, my mind creating memories.

    *The day that followed, I gave up Gibraltar...*
No, that's not how it was; it's how it could have been.
    The day was one of high professionalism,
and only once, after a strenuous session
when neither side would cede an inch,
did I catch her eye in an ambiguous glance,
a half-smile, after which I was more conciliatory.

    I needn't talk you through the day,
the meals, the unwanted entertainments.
After it all, the world shrank:
the two of us once more in my orange room.
But this time was all failure, permanent failure:
I think the previous night had broken something.

    I loved her, but my body refused
to act, to stiffen, to ready itself:
my penis lay like an ostrich chick,
all weak neck and closed mouth,
unable to bury its head in the ground.

And now she was angry,
urging me to perform like I had before,
claiming the rights she had bought with her body,
naughtily insistent, cajoling, mocking.
*Come on, time to pay your debt!*
    But everything in vain,
both kinds of assault, the subtle and the direct:
when the flesh is weak, the spirit is useless.

    I blushed, and was disconcerted:
shame fractured my willpower,
and a feedback loop of sheer terror
left me afraid and paralysed –
one past failure insisted on a failed present.

    She reached over to me,
began to stroke me and cajole:
rounded her hand around my sleeping member,
kissed it gently, blew on it
as though from dormant embers charming a fire.
    But, like I said, I was broken:
the soft air and even her muttered spells
did nothing to call the blood to my sex,
and in the midst of all her heat
I stayed cold and miserable, and shivered.

    *There's someone else… is there someone else?*
*Have you been working fast, tomcatting around*
*with other women from the delegation?*
*Are you just here to screw us all over,*
*cultural imperialism via your cock?*
*Whose bed did you crawl from to come to mine?*

I told her she was mistaken,
it was diplomacy itself kept me down:
the daily worry about how to meet the world,
the arguments, the threats, the papers
drawn up only to be torn apart again…
a thousand thousand aspects of my day job
that froze me at my night-time duties.
    She looked sceptical, and thought I was lying:
*You can't fool me; you can't fool love.*
*They say that love is blind, but they are lying:*
*Justice is blind, or Stevie Wonder.*
*Love itself has a hundred eyes.*
    *Come on, bring yourself back to this bed,*
*stop playing the Great Game and come back*
*to our little game, here, and now.*
    *If it is as you say, and your senses are frozen*
*from too much work and worry,*
*then just lay down your problems for a moment:*
*as soon as it's set aside, a trouble's weightless.*

    I flung myself back on the bed,
naked and hopeless,
and she was at its foot, equally naked,
walking from side to side of the room –
a sight that should have made any man perk up
(or any man's little man, for that matter).
    And nothing happened, and I started to cry,
the pathetic hot tears of a little old man
who cannot get what he wants.

    *It's not that my desire has failed,* I said.
*It is not that. I sat next to you this evening,*
*and when you turned your head*
*to your neighbour, and I saw the line*

*that runs from under your ear,*
*down your neck, and your jawline,*
*the sheer balanced heft of it, the delicacy…*
*I felt so much in love – and privileged*
*that I might later touch that neck –*
*my heart swelled and I felt nothing apart from love.*

    *And when you turned and spoke to me,*
*and I said something that made you laugh,*
*and your eyes sparked, you were truly amused…*
*Oh, this evening I was the happiest man*
*in either of our countries.*

    *No, my feelings are not to blame:*
*they have not changed, grow stronger even.*

    *It's age that is the problem, obdurate age:*
*these tools, this tool, has passed its sell-by date.*
*I've spent my life in the service of beauty,*
*but my weapons now are rusted.*
*Here's my rusty helmet, my rusty lance.*

    *Do what you will, but I am done:*
*there's nothing left after last night.*
*Last night itself was an aberration:*
*I am sorry for the intimacy between us.*


    She would not believe me,
and bent over one last time,
and whispered suggestions in my ear –
*Perhaps we could…? Would you like to…? –*
suggestions that in earlier years
would have caused me to growl like a tiger
and leap on her, and ravage her flesh,
and greet the morning sullied and joyous.
But that night: nothing. The Big Zero.

And when she saw all her effort,
her invitations to her own humiliation,
her nature and her arts all useless –
the member in question still lay quiescent
as though this were nothing to do with *him* –
then she threw herself on the bed next to me,
her hair untied and tangled over her sweating shoulders,
and cried herself a little, from frustration,
then laid her head on my spongy gut
looking away from me
and spoke her regret to my cock as follows:
   *Oh you, you used to make everything better.*
   *You used to be a treasure and a joy to me:*
   *how can I lament you, what tears can I shed,*
   *now that you no longer shed your tears?*
   *How can I memorialise you, who made me so happy –*
   *I always used to laugh after sex, the relief of it –*
   *what kind of a monument could I raise to you,*
   *now you can no longer raise yourself?*
   *How can I thank you for your service*
   *now that this will has come to nothing?*
   *A gilt carriage-clock would be traditional,*
   *or a card signed by everyone in the office…*
   *I loved you and your acolytes, I loved every inch of you.*
   *You took my mind off things, or put it on one thing,*
   *stayed with me through hours of pleasure and pain.*
   *You witnessed my most mysterious joys,*
   *had a front-row seat at half of them,*
   *or else stood guard to see no one disturbed us,*
   *willing at any moment to be called to the fray.*
   *My whim was a trumpet call, and where are you now?*
   *Where is your vigour, the way you would strike me*
   *over and again, soft blows that made me sigh?*

*Where is your rosy head, that would dip and disappear,*
*swallowed up, then return and dive again?*
    *Here you are, beaten, beaten down:*
*you used to be purple, now you are pale as milk,*
*as limp as nothing, limp as a boiled leek.*
    *I try everything, and you are insensible:*
*I pride myself that I'm quite good at this,*
*and even I, with all my charms, have failed.*
    *I weep for your death, oh poor pale penis:*
*if you can't do your job, you're as good as dead.*

    This public eulogy to my private parts
    made me uneasy, and I gave an awkward laugh:
    *Woman, wow, you've got it bad. I'm sorry,*
*but my old tool is only one of thousands.*
*Go on, be happy, move on to the next one,*
*there must be plenty more pricks in the sea.*
*So mine doesn't spark joy?*
*Kondo that fucker and move on.*

    She spun, faster than I'd seen her move before,
    and looked at me, true fury in her eyes.

    *Oh, you are wrong, you traitor, you foreigner!*
*I'm not sorry for myself, but for the whole collapsing world.*
    *You talk about intimacy: intimacy's nothing.*
*Does the fact that one drunken night*
*some dank pearl bulged at the end of a condom*
*give us any connection at all*
*beyond those small, fraught, gasping minutes?*
    *This isn't you and me; it's the way it's all disappearing.*
*If a prick doesn't work we're done for:*
*a symptom of how we're all –*
*you'll excuse the expression – fucked…*

*I came to the talks, but it wasn't a honey-trap,*
*just an idea that a happy man won't go to war:*
*procreation's important, everything's all on an edge,*
*we need to do what we can to calm down.*

    *Sex is a kind of diplomacy,*
*the way to draw two minds together*
*so closely that two souls become one flesh.*
*If there's no possibility of making love,*
*then beauty is worthless, male as well as female.*

    *The background to our lives can't be simple*
*unadorned self-interest, mechanics and wheels,*
*self-interest framed as debate, good people on both sides.*

    *With all the questions you came here to answer,*
*there is only self-interest in the face*
*of a greater, uncaring, guilty terror,*
*where sex won't help you, borders won't help you,*
*nothing will be redeemed from the general wreck.*

    *Oh, you can gather your nationalism,*
*gather your pretty memories of fucking me,*
*but moments you feel have been transcendent*
*won't save you when the seas start to rise.*

    *Debate? The debate between those who think*
*we should not burn the world, and those who say*
*we should carry on burning, that a result*
*of future burning will be a brand-new salve?*
*Debate? Debate that doesn't rise above:*
*'Sir, I'm no racist! My houseslave's black!'?*
*None of this is debate. I'm sick of diplomacy.*

    *When you think of all the good a prick can do,*
*and how it's always the old unchained,*
*sabre-rattling, dong-waving use it's put to...*

    *There are things to be said for living at the end*
*of an Empire – the chance of final synthesis,*
*of having literally the last word...*

*Though we have reached the point where even to say*
Future generations will condemn us
*is to speak with unwarranted optimism.*
    *I see children at play, the last-but-one issue of children:*
*beautiful, but the state of the current world*
*ruins everything, even beauty.*
*We are walking corpses, and this is regretful.*
    *Future aliens will try to piece together*
*who we were really, and why we fucked up so hard.*

    *I can say this too easy, the ease of words*
*parallel to their sweetness –*
*sticky, muddy words that I choke on,*
*even as they come with their retching fluidity.*
    *But they are my words, finally.*
    *Yes, I can have the last word, and my last word is this …*
*grow up, grow up and use your cock*
*for what it's meant for, not to think with.*
    *An unthinking penis, kept at work in bed,*
*will do more good than when frustrated,*
*filling a man's brain with boiling, aggressive sperm.*
    *If your prick is limp, your thoughts go elsewhere.*
    *Everything yields to a non-metaphorical penis*
*even the highest, most sacred things.*

And again, she apostrophised me down there,
one last farewell to the tool she was leaving:
    *Oh, penis! Weapons bow down before you,*
*calmly, without groans or resentment.*
    *Sword-blows are not more terrible than your anger.*
    *Wisdom herself, who would rule the world,*
*offers her hands to you, allows you to guide her.*
    *You bring so much happiness to the world:*
*virginity dies with a smile on her face,*

*slain by your wished-for stroke.*
   *You should not be like this old man's poor prick,*
*but stand courageous, and perform great tasks.*
   *Am I talking about the penis now,*
*or about what I want the penis to mean?*
*Art thou but a penis of the mind?*
*You suffer, penis, principle of courage,*
*as you make your way through storms, ambushes,*
*traps, loss and bitter argument.*
   *But the calm after the storm,*
*the hero's journey ending when all the traps are past …*
*you alone can provoke the perfect sadness,*
*the love that speaks its name,*
*the union built on bricks of sex,*
*that calms the tiger and the lion in their rages.*
   *Invincible penis! Invincible idea of the penis!*
*Patient, conquering, desiring to be conquered.*
*World gathering to a head,*
*willing to defeat and be defeated.*
*Your anger is brief,*
*your pity is great,*
*joy flows through you.*
*And even without your power,*
*your purpose, if not your use, remains.*

   After this weird speech, a kind of last rites to my cock,
she laid her head back on my arm.
I didn't speak, the light had faded completely,
and in the distance the noise of the city was dead.
We slept a while, and when I awoke,
she had silently left me, leaving the scene of a crime.
Nothing to remind me of her,
no sign she had even existed,

except a single twisted Tristram Shandy hair
against the white bathroom tiles.


I opened the curtain; the sky was full of storm-light;
migrating birds flew past, an arrow pointing nowhere.

VI.

Oh, enough words, please, old man,
haven't you said your piece, little Homunculus?
We've seen your shame in the round;
to carry on would be its own shame.
All life is the set-up: the punchline's obvious.
The path we travel is always the same.
Old men tread it, boys; rich and poor: the same ground;
Better to hurry than to dawdle.
    Live ironically! The best we may
pray for is some vast plague.
I am a corpse already mourned.
My prick may be dead; my poems live still.
    I'm nearly done, and thank you for caring.
*Was that the future, or just a red herring?*

*Obliged to you for hearing me, and now*
*Old Homunculus ain't got nothing more to say.*

AFTERWORD

This is a long poem, conceived and planned over the course of about two years, and written up from my notes at, for me, frantic speed, over the Easter of 2019.

It was largely inspired by the *Elegies* of Maximian, or Maximianus, a writer who has been identified as 'in some sort, the last of the Roman poets'. He wrote probably around 550 AD.

I first heard of Maximian via W.H. Auden, who gives Maximian as the last entry in his list of Roman poets in his 1966 essay 'The Fall of Rome': 'Finally, in the sixth century after the West has fallen, one really remarkable poet, Maximian.' Susceptible that I am, this phrase, 'really remarkable', was encouragement enough for me to seek him out.

Helen Waddell, in *The Wandering Scholars*, calls Maximian's *Elegies* 'one of the strangest documents of the human mind: Ecclesiastes without its austere reconciliation: the "*ossa arida* of the Valley of Dead Pleasures", but no breath from the four winds will blow upon these slain [...] an autobiography, written with a terrible sincerity, redeemed from over-intimacy by the inhumanity of the art'. I concur.

Maximian's elegies are a total of 686 lines long: the current poem, if my word-counter is to be trusted, is around 2,200 lines. I state statistics – boring! – to support my notion that this is not really a translation, or maybe more than a translation: I certainly don't think of it as a straight translation. I worked with the Latin text, a French translation (Désiré Nisard?) from 1850, and L.R. Lind's 1988 English version of the poems, but I allowed myself the freedom to alter and expand the text and my responses to it as I saw fit. A long poem whose protagonist is my version of Maximian's protagonist, perhaps. Worth noting that neither of those people is me.

Longer passages in italics, except where italics indicate speech, tend to be quotations from other sources.

As well as factual notes, there should be space made here for gratitude. I am grateful to have been granted a month's writing time as a Hawthornden Fellow in March-April 2019, during which the bulk of this poem was sketched out.

Thanks are due to many people, but in particular to my wife Marian, whose constant support and encouragement, as well as her nice capacity to assess when I am being stupid, has helped immeasurably with the completion of this project.